For Tom & Barbara
with love.

Richey

FURTHER
DEPARTURES

A Collection of Quotations
Compiled by
Richard Kehl

GREEN TIGER PRESS, INC

Text copyright © 1990 by Richard Kehl
Cover pictures copyright © 1990 by Richard Kehl
Green Tiger Press, Inc., 435 East Carmel Street
San Marcos, California 92069-4362
ISBN 0-88138-138-1
First Edition
10 9 8 7 6 5 4 3 2 1

And the end of all our exploring
Will be to arrive where we started.
And know the place for the first time.

T.S. Eliot

Poetry heals the wounds inflicted by
reason.

Novalis

In heaven an angel is nobody in particular.

George Bernard Shaw

The Future is something which everyone
reaches at the rate of sixty minutes an hour.

C.S. Lewis

I never practice; I always play.

Wanda Landowska

The key to success is simple. Make people
dream.

Gerard de Nerval

Racing is strictly art for art's sake. There
are few things more useless than a race car.

Sam Posey

I have a sailboat of sinking water.

Anonymous child

In 1802 Kant discharged Lampe, the faithful servant who had been with him for years. But he could not dismiss him from his mind and this began to trouble him greatly. He therefore made an entry in his memorandum book: "Remember, from now on the name of Lampe must be completely forgotten."

"One and one make two. That's great. What's a two?"

Bill Cosby

The energy you use to turn a single page of a book is more than all the radio telescopes have collected since the beginning of radio astronomy.

Jocelyn Ball, Burnell Judson, and Horace Freeland

If it's not one thing, it's not another.

Cooper Edens

Truth is in all things, even partly, in error.

Jean luc Godard

As James Reston of the New York Times says: "Where you stand depends on where you sit."

I have on my wall a great quote from Sir Laurence Olivier. He and Charlton Heston had done a play somewhere about twenty-five years ago, and they'd gotten slaughtered. Heston said, "Well, I guess you've just got to forget the bad reviews." And Olivier said, "No, you've got to forget the good ones."

William Goldman

The moment is the only thing that counts.

Jean Cocteau

"I've got ground glass in my bones," she said.

Gabriel Maria Marquez

Deserve your dream.

Octavio Paz

A well-known physicist in Britain once told Wolfgang Kohler, "We often talk about the three B's, the Bus, the Bath, and the Bed. That is where the great discoveries are made in our science."

Julian Jaynes

I'm tired of all this nonsense about beauty
being only skin-deep. That's deep enough.
What do you want— an adorable pancreas?

Jean Kerr

I say to my breath once again, little
breath come from in front of me, go away
behind me, row me quietly now, as far as
you can, for I am an abyss that I am trying
to cross.

W.S. Merwin

Granted, we die for good. Life, then, is
largely a thing of happens to like, not
should.

Wallace Stevens

I know I was writing stories when I was
five. I don't know what I did before that. Just
loafed I suppose.

P.G. Wodehouse

No mistake's made once: that's an
adventure.

David Mus

The chains that bind us most closely are the ones we have broken.

Antonio Porchia

Somebody's boring me ... I think it's me.

Dylan Thomas

There are no secrets except the secrets that keep themselves.

George Bernard Shaw

At a performance of Pulcinella, Jean Hugo was sitting next to Picasso in Misia Sert's box. Suddenly, Picasso turned to him and asked: "So, are you still painting by hand?" Hugo would be puzzled by it for years.

Questions are fiction, and answers are anything from more fiction to science-fiction.

Saul Steinberg

Half of everything you've learned is wrong--but I don't know which half.

Anonymous

Beware of losing what isn't in your head.

John Cage

The immediate is chance. At the same
time it is definitive. What I want is the
definitive by chance.

Jean luc Godard

I am homesick for a country. I have never
been there. I shall never go there. But where
the clouds remember me distinctly.

Hilde Domin

So you're the kind of vegetarian that only
eats roses.

Leonard Cohen

Remarks are not literature.

Gertrude Stein

In one of his autobiographical works, the English author Augustus John Cuthbert Hare described the experience of a certain lady who awoke in the middle of the night with the sense that someone else was in her room. The sound of footsteps going to and fro across the room and the impression of hands moving over the bed terrified the poor lady so much that she fainted. Only when morning came was it discovered that the butler had walked in his sleep and set the table for fourteen places upon her bed.

Even stones have a love, a love that seeks the ground.

Meister Eckhart

I force myself into self-contradiction to avoid following my taste.

Marcel Duchamp

Dr. Adrian Kantrowitz feels that many times it will not be necessary to remove the whole heart in a transplant operation. "We can leave it at least for sentimental value," he said.

Newspaper

Why is it better to love than be loved? It is surer.

Sacha Guitry

Alifano: But why is time ungraspable?
Borges: Undoubtedly, because time is made up of memory ... And that memory is made up largely of forgetfulness.

"Which foolish man was it who said love was simple?" she murmured. "Ah, yes, it was Rodolphe. But which Rodolphe?"

Leon Garfield

The question is how immediately are you going to say yes to no matter what unpredictability.

John Cage

Each second we live is a new and unique moment of the universe--And what do we teach our children in school? We teach them that two and two make four and that Paris is the capital of France. When will we also teach them what they are? We should say to each of them ... "In all the world there is no other child exactly like you."

Author Unknown

... a final comfort that is small, but not cold: the heart is the only broken instrument that works.

T.E. Kalem

But I mark my beginning as a professional biographer from the day when my bank bounced a cheque because it was inadvertently dated 1772.

R. Holmes

Vision is the art of seeing things invisible.

Jonathan Swift

When in doubt, tell the truth.

Mark Twain

I hold this to be the highest task of a bond between two people: that each should stand guard over the solitude of the other.

Rainer Maria Rilke

Whether you think you can or think you can't, you're right.

Henry Ford

In heaven, everyone will be the age when they were most happy.

Author Unknown

I detest my past and anyone else's. I detest resignation, patience, professional heroism, and obligatory beautiful feelings. I also detest the decorative arts, folklore, advertising, voices making announcements, aerodynamism, boy scouts, the smell of mothballs, events of the moment, and drunken people.

René Magritte

It infuriates me to be wrong when I know I'm right.

Jean Molière

I had always liked the story about Johnny Kerr, the pro basketball player with bad legs who set a record for consecutive games. Clearly, he played in pain. After he had set the record, he was asked how he could play hurt night after night. His answer: "I tell my legs lies."

Love is a hole in the heart.

Ben Hecht

A sea which is a mistake is impossible.

Odysseus Elytis

An author who claims to write for posterity must be a bad one. We should never know for whom we write.

E.M. Cioran

...one bright, moonlit night a messenger thrust a note into the ante-room where I was staying. On a sheet of magnificent scarlet paper I read the words, 'there is nothing.' It was the moonlight that made this so delightful; I wonder whether I would have enjoyed it at all on a rainy night.

The Pillow Book of Sei Shonagon

Send forget-me-nots anonymously.

Author Unknown

And curious creatures that we are, in every sense of the word. Not only are we the sole animal in all of nature capable of believing in Santa Claus, we are also the only one that can come to grasp with the unpleasant truth that he doesn't exist.

Jon Franklin

Think before you think!

Stanislaw Lec

Everyone is a genius at least once a year. The real geniuses simply have their bright ideas closer together.

George Lichtenberg

Existence is no more than a flaw in the perfection of non-existence.

Paul Valery

Your eyes. It's a day's work just looking into them.

Laurie Anderson

Shakespeare couldn't have written Shakespeare if he'd had a typewriter.

Author Unknown

Nevertheless, Debussy clearly played his own pieces straight. Misty music to sound misty must be played without mist.

Ned Rorem

Colette on her divan: "Oh! How I'd like to feel the cold belly of a little frog on each hand."

I refuse to admit I'm more than fifty-two, even if that does make my sons illegitimate.

Lady Astor

James McNeill Whistler ... his reply to the gushing lady who said that she had just come up from the country along the Thames, "and there was an exquisite haze in the atmosphere which reminded me so much of some of your little things. It was really a perfect series of Whistlers." "Yes, madame," he returned with the utmost gravity: "Nature is creeping up."

Hesketh Pearson

Have you seen my memory
The flame far from the candles.

W.S. Merwin

If silence is everywhere it is because it is about time.

den Boer

Be patient toward all that is unsolved in your heart and try to love the questions themselves. Do not seek the answers, which cannot be given you, because you would not be able to live them. And the point is, to live everything. *Live* the questions now. Perhaps you will then gradually, without noticing it, live along some distant day into the answer.

Rainer Maria Rilke

And if you still find something, you have not lost everything. You still have to lose something.

Antonio Porchia

Consideration—a nice word meaning putting two stars together.

Buckminster Fuller

One of the oddest things in life, I think, is the thing one remembers.

Agatha Christie

Such simplicity cannot be taught. But it can be denied and lost.

Elizabeth Janeway

...as for logic, it's in the eye of the logician.

Gloria Steinem

One always has to spoil a picture a little bit, in order to finish it.

Eugene Delacroix

It was chilling to realize that the sentimental qualities most valued between people, like loyalty, constancy, and affection, are the ones most likely to impede change.

Ted Simon

Love is an act of endless forgiveness, a tender look which becomes a habit.

Peter Ustinov

From my disinherited mother I learned to stay alive by dreaming myself into existence—from her I learned that *everything* is real. It was a lesson of enormous value to me.

Jamake Highwater

Each act is virgin, even the repeated one.

René Char

Polanski and I discuss a shot of the advancing English army and he asks, "Should they move right to left across the frame, or left to right?" I rashly say, "does it matter?" "Of course it matters," he says. "To the Western eye, easy or successful movement is left to right, difficult or failed movement is right to left." He sends out for a children's comic to prove his point. On the first page a canoe is shooting the rapids left to right, and a man is climbing a mountain right to left.

Kenneth Tynan

There is poetry as soon as we realize that we possess nothing.

John Cage

As a special treat, a teacher took her class to visit the Museum of Natural History. The children returned home very excitedly, and rushing into his house, one of the little boys greeted his mother exuberantly, saying, "What do you think we did today, Mother! The teacher took us to a dead circus."

Author Unknown

May I ask you a highly personal question? It's what life does all the time.

Kurt Vonnegut

The day in the woods I took a compass
was the day I got lost for sure.

John Cage

They have stopped deceiving you, not
loving you. And to you it seems that they
have stopped loving you.

Antonio Porchia

In the late 1600's the finest instruments
originated from three rural families whose
workshops were side by side in the Italian
village of Cremona. First were the Amatis, and
outside their shop hung a sign: "The best
violins in all Italy." Not to be outdone, their
next door neighbors, the family Guarnerius,
hung a bolder sign proclaiming: "The Best
Violins In All The World!" At the end of the
street was the workshop of Anton Stradivarius,
and on its front door was a simple notice
which read: "The best violins on the block."

Freda Bright

To see an aquarium, better not be a fish.

Andre Malraux

One must stop before one has finished.

Barbara Tuchman

The art of love? It's knowing how to join
the temperament of a vampire to the
discretion of an anemone.

E.M. Cioran

Reality is not what it is. It consists of the
many realities which it can be made into.

Wallace Stevens

Who can tell the dancer from the dance?

William Butler Yeats

My grandfather told me once that the best
map is one that points to which way is north
and shows you how much water is in your way.

Stephen King

I think we are responsible for the universe,
but that doesn't mean we decide anything.

René Magritte

If Galileo had said in verse that the world
moved, the inquisition might have let him
alone.

Thomas Hardy

My good friend Jacques Monod spoke
often of the randomness of the cosmos. He
believed everything in existence occurred by
pure chance with the possible exception of
his breakfast, which he felt certain was made
by his housekeeper.

Woody Allen

I took the Second World War in school, but
I can't remember how it came out.

Anonymous Student

You phone the Time Lady and listen to her
tell the minutes and seconds ... she distinctly
names the present moment, never slipping
into the past or sliding into the future.

Maxine Hong Kingston

To make creative breakthroughs, or, as
Buckminster Fuller called them, intuitively
inadvertent cul-de-sacs.

If one tells the truth, one is sure, sooner or
later, to be found out.

Oscar Wilde

What is irritating about love is that it is a crime that requires an accomplice.

Charles Baudelaire

My time reversal experiments are proceeding more slowly than I anticipated.

Anonymous Scientist at the Univiversity of Washington

He thought that she must have a lovely, an exquisitely beautiful skeleton. Every bone was in place, as finely finished as a violin. Boris imagined that he might be very happy with her, that he might even fall in love with her, could he have her in her beautiful bones alone ... Many human relations, he thought, would be infinitely easier if they could be carried out in the bones only.

Isak Dinesen

It's a love story. No one's ahead.

Anonymous

We are two mirrors crossing their swords.

Octavio Paz

The chief cause of problems is solutions.

Eric Sevareid

When the Duke of Wellington was asked by an admirer, "How did you really manage to beat Napoleon?" he replied simply, "Well, I'll tell you. Bonaparte's plans were made in wire, mine were made in string."

Life is what happens to you while you're busy making other plans.

John Lennon

Time is a great teacher, but unfortunately it kills all its pupils.

Hector Berlioz

If one looks at a thing with the intentions of trying to discover what it means, one ends up no longer seeing the thing itself, but thinking of the question that has been raised. One cannot speak about mystery; one must be seized by it.

René Magritte

You've got to outlast yourself.

Clint Eastwood

Be ahead of all parting, as though it already were behind you.

Rainer Maria Rilke

Love is much nicer to be in than an automobile accident, a tight girdle, a higher tax bracket, or a holding pattern over Philadelphia.

Judith Viors

Whatever it is, I'm against it.

Groucho Marx

It is a profoundly erroneous truism, repeated by all the copy books, and by eminent people when they are making speeches, that we should cultivate the habit of thinking what we are doing. The precise opposite is the case.

Alfred North Whitehead

Everything that happens is at once natural and inconceivable.

E.M. Cioran

The painter and the painter contemplating his painting are not the same man.

Joan Miro

The sole cause of man's unhappiness is that he does not know how to stay quietly in his room.

Blaise Pascal

Any time that is not spent on love is
wasted.

Tasso

...from the Persian monarch who, having
to adjudicate upon two poems, caused the
one to be read to him, and at once, without
ado, awarded the prize to the other.

Sir Arthur Quiller-Couch

"Down with style!" Picasso had
proclaimed to Malraux. "Does God have
style? He made the guitar, the harlequin, the
dachshund, the cat, the owl, the dove. The
elephant and the whale, fine, but the
elephant and the squirrel? A real
hodgepodge!"

Practice makes imperfect.

Ned Rorem

Anyone who can handle a needle
convincingly can make us see a thread
which is not there.

E.H. Gombrich

If the doors of perception were cleansed, everything would appear to man as it is, infinite.

William Blake

Sighs are air, and go to the air, tears are water, and go to the sea. Tell me fair one, if you know: when love is forgotten, where can it go?

Gustave Adolfo Bacquer

In this story, the boy Chi Po is taking painting lessons from the sorcerer Bu Fu. At one point, Bu Fu is looking at Chi Po's painting and says: "No, No! You have merely painted what *is*. Anybody can paint what is! The real secret is to paint what isn't." Upon which Chi Po was very puzzled and said, "But what is there that isn't?"

Oscar Mandel

No one shows a child the sky.

African Proverb

Catching a fly ball is a pleasure, but knowing what to do with it is a business.

Tommy Henrich of the New York Yankees

Two doctors from Derby reported in 1981 about a woman, blind since the age of 27, who began to suffer deafness a few years later. "I can no longer hear the silence of lamp-posts," she said one day.

Author Unknown

A book is a mirror: when a monkey looks in, no apostle can look out.

George C. Lichtenberg

In a journal entry for January 8, 1966, Joseph Cornell asserted that he lived one day ahead of conventional time.

Everything exists, nothing has value.

E.M. Forster

I am not interested in grasping precisely a man I know. I am interested only in exaggerating him precisely.

Elias Canetti

According to Paley, the Bishop was once impatient at the slowness of his Carlisle printer, "Why does not my book make its appearance?" he said to the printer. "My Lord, I am extremely sorry, but we have been obliged to send to Glasgow for a pound of parentheses."

Boswell of Dr. Edmund Low

In order to reach the truth, it is necessary, once in one's life, to put everything in doubt—so far as possible.

Descartes

If you haven't all the things you want, be grateful for the things you don't have that you didn't want.

Anonymous

Nowhere one goes will one ever be away enough from wherever one was.

Robert Creeley

What words say does not last. The words last. Because words are always the same, and what they say is never the same.

Antonio Porchia

At the end of every forget is a remember.

Lonny Brown

Fred Astaire once said to Jack Lemmon, "You're at a level where you can only afford one mistake. The higher up you go, the more mistakes you're allowed. Right at the top, if you make enough of them, it's considered to be your style."

Quenton Crisp

It is a sin peculiar to man to hate his victim.

Tacitus

Strange how much you've got to know before you know how little you know.

Author Unknown

Thomas Edison lost much of his hearing at an early age. But I just read he and his wife attended stage plays. How did he hear the actor? His wife fingertipped key lines of dialogue in Morse code on his knee.

Didn't I tell you he taught her Morse code? Then tapped out his marriage proposal in her hand? She tapped back her acceptance.

Newspaper

You are always in the beginning of some prophecy that you will not believe to save your life.

Jay Wright

"What is the answer?" asked Gertrude Stein on her deathbed. There was silence. "Well, then what is the question?"—and she died.

Astronomy is the study of telescopes.

Anonymous

If you give what can be taken, you are not really giving. Take what you are given, not what you want to be given. Give what cannot be taken.

Idries Shah

How to the invisible I hired myself to learn...that has as its last and seventh rule: the submission to chance.

Charles Simic

The old Duc de Broglie, reminiscing in company about memorable letters he had received, recalled "The one that gave me the greatest satisfaction was one I got from a very lovely lady. It consisted of only one word."

"And that was?" said one of the guests.

"Friday."

W. Scholz

You can't be lonely on the sea—you're too alone.

Tania Aebi

Progress in itself is not always positive. Disease progresses.

Ned Rorem

When I was in India I met and conversed briefly with Shri Atmananda Guru of Trivandrum, and the question he gave me to consider was this: Where are you between two thoughts?

Joseph Campbell

Nothing is more vain than to die for love. What we ought to do is live.

Marcel Camus

He found an enormous old umbrella in the trunk. The bright satin material had been eaten away by the moths. "Look what's left of our circus clown's umbrella," said the Colonel with one of his old phrases. Above his head a mysterious system of little metal rods opened. "The only thing it's good for now is to count the stars."

Gabriel Garcia Marquez

"When one of us dies, I'll move to the Riviera" said a woman to her husband when she saw the beautiful Mediterranean coast.

For something to be a masterpiece you have to have enough time to talk when you have nothing to say.

John Cage

It is the end of importance.

Jill Johnston

Perhaps all pleasure is only relief.

William Burroughs

Einstein was a late talker, his parents were worried. At last, at the supper table one night, he broke his silence to say, "The soup is too hot." Greatly relieved, his parents asked why he had never said a word before. Albert replied, "Because up to now everything was in order."

Above all, do not plant me in your heart. I grow much too fast.

Author Unknown

One must have teeth. Then love's like biting into an orange when the juice squirts in your teeth.

Bertolt Brecht

I keep coming back to you in my head, but you couldn't know that, and I have no carbons.

Adrienne Rich

I read somewhere that Rubens said students should not draw from life, but draw from all the great classic casts. Then you really get the measure of them, you really know what to do. And *then*, put in your own dimples. Isn't that marvelous!

Willem DeKooning

Concentrate, don't embroider.

Spencer Tracy

Researchers at Bell Laboratories estimate that there is more information in a weekly edition of The New York Times than a person in the sixteenth century processed in a lifetime.

Lawrence Shainberg

Isn't it amazing the way the future succeeds in creating an appropriate past?

John Leonard

Few people have the imagination for reality.

Johann Wolfgang von Goethe

I am the shadow my words cast.

Octavio Paz

I can't recall who first pointed out that the word "explain" means literally to *flatten out.*

Philip Slater

You find out that the universe is a system that creeps up on itself and says "Boo!" and then laughs at itself for jumping.

Alan Watts

John Dewey was nearer the mark when he described thought as 'active uncertainty.'

Brodsky returned to the serious study of English during his period of exile. Equipped only with a paperback anthology of English and American poetry and an English-Russian dictionary, he spent long evenings puzzling over the verses of Dylan Thomas, W. H. Auden, Eliot, Yeats, and Wallace Stevens. His technique was simple: he made literal translations of the first and last stanzas and then tried to 'imagine' what, poetically speaking, should come in between!

George Kline

Have you noticed there is never any third act in a nightmare? They bring you to a climax of terror and then leave you there.

Max Beerbohm

The composer-as-teacher runs a danger.
Teachers repeat themselves. After the first
year they not only believe what they say,
they believe *in* what they say, so they say
forever the same thing.

Ned Rorem

When dealing with the insane, the best
method is to pretend to be sane.

Hermann Hesse

All the things one has forgotten scream for
help in dreams.

Elias Canetti

No word meaning 'art' occurs in Aivilik,
nor does 'artist;' there are only people. Nor
is any distinction made between utilitarian
and decorative objects. The Aivilik say
simply, "A man should do all things
properly." Art to the Aivilik is an act, not an
object—a ritual, not a possession.

Enchantment is destroyed by vagueness,
and mystery exists only in precise things.

Jean Cocteau

Order, unity, and continuity are human inventions, just as truly as catalogues and encyclopedias.

Bertrand Russell

In 1953, Jack Lemmon came to Hollywood to make his first film. The director was George Cukor. During the first rehearsals Cukor, after each of Lemmon's tries, would cry, "Less, less, less!" Lemmon, frustrated and bewildered, finally broke out with "Don't you want me to act at *all*?" "Dear boy," said Cukor, "you're beginning to understand."

To name an object is largely to destroy poetic enjoyment.

Stéphane Mallarmé

First young lady: "Have you seen Omnibook? It takes five or six books and boils them down. That way you can read them all in one evening."

Second young lady: "I wouldn't like it. Seems to me it would just spoil the movie for you."

Author Unknown

By the time you read this, it is dark on the next page.

W.S. Merwin

I wouldn't have believed it if I hadn't seen it. (But more neurophysiologically precise to say) I wouldn't have seen it at all, if I hadn't already believed it in the first place.

Lyall Watson

I have calculated that if I see a film that lasts an hour, I am in fact plunged into absolute blackness for twenty minutes. In making a film, I am thus guilty of fraud.

Ingmar Bergman

Realism is a corruption of reality.

Wallace Stevens

The formula 'Two and two make five' is not without its attractions.

Fyodor Dostoevsky

Until death, it is all life.

Miguel de Cervantes

A true poet does not bother to be poetical.
Nor does a nursery gardener scent his roses.

Jean Cocteau

An art dealer bought a canvas signed
'Picasso' and travelled all the way to Cannes
to discover whether it was genuine. Picasso
was working in his studio. He cast a single
look at the canvas and said, "It's a fake." A
few months later the dealer bought another
Canvas signed 'Picasso.' Again he travelled
to Cannes and again Picasso, after a single
glance, grunted: "It's a fake." "But cher
maitre," expostulated the dealer, "it so
happens that I saw you with my own eyes
working on this picture several years ago."
Picasso shrugged: "I often paint fakes."

Arthur Koestler

Atoms are so small and there are so many
of them. For example, in your last breath it
is almost certain that you have inhaled at
least one atom from the dying breath of
Julius Caesar.

Heinz Pagels

Real books should be the offspring not of daylight and casual talk but of darkness and silence.

Marcel Proust

While I thought that I was learning how to live, I have been learning how to die.

Leonardo Da Vinci

Reality is only a Rorschach ink-blot, you know.

Alan Watts

Reminder: What am I doing on a level of consciousness where this is real?

Anonymous

All the information I have about myself is from forged documents.

Vladimir Nabokov

Where are our great forgetters—who will teach us to forget about such and such a part of the world—where is the Christopher Columbus to whom once again we will owe the forgetting of an entire vast continent of creation—to lose—but to lose truly—to make room for discovery.

Guillaume Apollinaire

Jean Gabin used to have a clause in his contract stipulating that he'd never have to open a door or bend over in any of his pictures.

It would have been more logical if silent pictures had grown out of the talkies instead of the other way around.

Mary Pickford

Meeting his old rival Lord Monboddo in an Edinburgh street shortly after the publication of *Elements of Criticism*, Lord Kames inquired whether Lord Monboddo had read it. "I have not, my Lord," was the response. "You write a great deal faster than I am able to read."

Lord Henry Home Kames

Matisse was accused of doing things any child could do, and he answered, very cheerfully, "Yes, but not what you could do."

Allan Kaprow

But they are useless. They can only give you answers.

Picasso, about computers

Our only security is our ability to change.

John Lilly

The physicist Leo Szilard once announced to his friend Hans Bethe that he was thinking of keeping a diary: "I don't intend to publish it: I am merely going to record the facts for the information of God." "Don't you think God knows the facts?" Bethe asked. "Yes," said Szilard. "He knows the facts, but he does not know *this version of the facts.*"

It is what you read when you don't have to that determines what you will be when you can't help it.

Oscar Wilde

Works of art can wait: indeed, they do nothing but that and do it passionately.

Rainer Maria Rilke

If I had to give young writers advice, I'd say don't listen to writers talking about writing.

Lillian Hellman

When I have arranged a bouquet, in order to paint it, I go around to the side that I have not looked at.

Jean Renoir

If you think you're boring your audience, go slower not faster.

Gustav Mahler

A stitch in time would have confused Einstein.

Anonymous

Biologists have suggested that the universe, and the living forms it contains, are based on chance, but not on accident.

Jeremy Campbell

I know poetry is indispensable, but to what?

Jean Cocteau

This is either a forgery or a damn clever original!

Frank Sullivan

Rossini to Louis Engel: When I was writing
the Chorus in G Minor, I suddenly dipped my
pen into the medicine bottle instead of the
ink: I made a blot, and when I dried it with
sand (blotting paper had not been invented
then) it took the form of a natural, which
instantly gave me the idea of the effect
which the change from G Minor to G Major
would make, and to this blot all the effect—if
any—is due.

My grandfather always said that living is
like licking honey off a thorn.

Louis Adamic

My green thumb came only as a result of
the mistakes I made while learning to see
things from the plant's point of view.

H. Fred Ale

I think it's better when things aren't brand
new. It's less tiring for the eyes.

Jean Renoir

We all know that Art is not truth. Art is a lie that makes us realize truth, at least the truth that is given us to understand. The artist must know the manner whereby to convince others of the truthfulness of his lies.

Pablo Picasso

It's not that I'm afraid to die, I just don't want to be there when it happens.

Woody Allen

We believe as much as we can. We would believe everything if we could.

William James

While I stood there I saw more than I can tell and I understood more than I saw.

Black Elk

It is not only the most difficult thing to know oneself, but the most inconvenient one, too.

H.W. Shaw

There is no truth. There is only perception.

Gustave Flaubert

The rules are simple — start on dry land, finish on dry land.

Mike Read, King of the English Channel

One thinks one is tracing the outline of the thing's nature over and over again, and one is merely tracing round the frame through which we look at it.

Ludwig Wittgenstein

If it weren't for Edison, we'd be watching TV by candlelight.

Anonymous

I dwell in possibility.

Emily Dickinson

If you had to save your works from a fire, which would you save? "Possibly none of them. What am I going to need them for? I would rather like to save a girl ... or a good collection of detective stories, ...Which would entertain me much more than my own poetry.

asked of Pablo Neruda

An idea isn't responsible for the people who believe in it.

Don Marquis

It is impossible, claims Auden, to imagine oneself as either more or less imaginative than, in fact, one is.

Ned Rorem

Our poetry now is the realization that we possess nothing. Anything therefore is a delight and thus need not fear its loss. We need not destroy the past. It is gone.

John Cage

Now I don't know which way to be. Absent-minded or respectful.

Pablo Neruda

One of the Second Republic's most grandiose ideas had been to establish a Museum of Copies in Paris, which could reproduce the best paintings of the whole world, and in 1851 four painters were dispatched to copy the works in the National Gallery in London.

Theodore Zeldin

My husband is so promiscuous that sometimes I'm not even sure who the father of our second child is.

Letter to Ann Landers

The fact is, I still work attempting to be invisible. Often, I have to start off attempting to do something by slipping into another consciousness that allows me to be the spectator while I'm working, so that there's at least an audience of one. And sometimes *that* can be a crowd.

Robert Rauschenberg

Grading is degrading.

Richard Kehl

If love is the answer, could you rephrase the question?

Lily Tomlin

Reason and justice tell me there's more love for humanity in electricity and steam than in chastity and vegetarianism.

Anton Chekhov

All good art is an indiscretion.

Tennessee Williams

When we came in she had her chair sideways, by the window, looking out at the snow, and she said, without even looking up to know that it was us, that the doctor had said that sitting and staring at the snow was a waste of time. She should get involved in something. She laughed and told us it wasn't a waste of time. It would be a waste of time just to stare at snowflakes, but she was counting, and even that might be a waste of time, but she was only counting the ones that were just alike.

Ann Beattie

The mind cannot possibly repeat itself.

Paul Valery

The great thing about human language is that it prevents us from sticking to the matter at hand.

Lewis Thomas

I don't have any ideas that are more than seven hundred words long.

Anonymous Columnist

Feeling that he must run and that he will take root forever and stand, does both at once, and neither, grows blind, and then sees everything, steps and becomes a man of stars instead.

James Dickey

He kept, as it were, a harem of words, to which he was constant and absolutely faithful. Some he favoured more than others, but he neglected none. He used them more often out of compliment than of necessity.

Alice Meynell, of Swineburne

People love chopping wood. In this activity one immediately sees results.

Albert Einstein

Complete possession is proved only by giving. All you are unable to give possesses you.

Andre Gide

A man marries to have a home, but also because he doesn't want to be bothered with sex and all that sort of thing.

W. Somerset Maugham

Next to the wound, what women make best is the bandage.

Jules Barbey d'Aurevilly

I find the childlikeness of genius in a lovely vignette Sjoman evokes for us: Ingmar Bergman and Nykvist looking at a somber Northern landscape together and Ingmar exclaiming, "Look at that! The entire scale of grey!" It takes a very sensitive man to perceive the entire scale of grey; but it takes a spontaneous child to exclaim about it with uninhibited joy.

I owe my solitude to other people.

Alan Watts

Millions and millions of years would still not give me half enough time to describe that tiny instant of all eternity when you put your arms around me and I put my arms around you.

Jacques Prévert

Cezanne averred he didn't need to take a vacation from painting his famous still lifes of fruit: he got all the excitement he could stand from the nuance of moving his easel a few inches.

To understand is almost the opposite of existing.

George Poulet

Die in your thoughts every morning and you will no longer fear death.

Hagakure

Flowers are without hope. Because hope is tomorrow and flowers have no tomorrow.

Antonio Porchia

A man is rich in proportion to the number of things he can afford to let alone.

Henry David Thoreau

Never play cards with a man called Doc: never eat at a place called Mom's: never go to bed with a woman who has more troubles than you have.

Nelson Algren

The Andromeda nebula is a beautiful pinwheel of stars and luminous clouds of gas. It is the large galaxy closest to our own. A friend of mine once showed a photograph of the Andromeda galaxy to the art director of a magazine on which he was working. The art director said: "That's gorgeous! But tell me. Can we get a shot of it from another angle?"

Author Unknown

Marriage is a wonderful invention: then again, so is a bicycle repair kit.

Billy Connolly

Her clothes have no buttons. There are two missing from my jacket. This lady and I are almost of the same religion.

Guillaume Appollinaire

If you don't make mistakes, you're not working on hard enough problems. And that's a big mistake.

F. Wikzek

As one scholar aptly put it, in many non-Western cultures they don't tell you what time it is: they tell you what kind of time it is.

Thomas Cottle and Stephen Klineberg

A mind all logic is like a knife all blade. It makes the hand bleed that uses it.

Rabindranath Tagore

Education is what remains after one has forgotten what one has learned in school.

Albert Einstein

The great mathematician David Hilbert praised a new student of his who seemed to show great promise. Some time later Ernst Cassirer asked him what had happened to this student. Hilbert replied, "Oh, he did not have enough imagination to be a mathematician, so he became a poet!"

Thoughts are in a hollow space in the heart, one inch square.

Chinese Proverb

A happy marriage is a long conversation which always seems too short.

Andre Maurois

The meaning of music lies not in the fact that it is too vague for words, but that it is too precise for words.

Felix Mendelssohn

Men live by forgetting—women live on memories.

T.S. Eliot

Truth is a great flirt.

Franz Liszt

I must have a prodigious quantity of mind: it takes me as much as a week sometimes to make it up.

Mark Twain

A visitor to Niels Bohr's country cottage, noticing a horseshoe hanging on the wall, teased the eminent scientist about this ancient superstition. "Can it be that you, of all people, believe it will bring you luck?" "Of course not," replied Bohr, "but I understand it brings you luck whether you believe or not."

God made everything out of nothing, but the nothingness shows through.

Paul Valery

Why must one always potter around in a garden? Can't you potter around in an armchair as well? I did once, confessed Snubbers moodily ... Gad, sir, what a wildcat she was! He chewed his wad of carbon paper reminiscently.

S.J. Perelman

A mirror dreams only of another mirror.

Anna Akhmatova

When our hands are alone, they open, like faces. There is no shore to their opening.

Author Unknown

It's useless to play lullabies for those who cannot go to sleep.

John Cage

Robert Graves said: Imagine that you're dreaming.

The price of passion is no passion.

John Fowles

By the time I was three, I was spending every waking moment at the keyboard, standing, placing my hands on the keyboard and pushing notes. And I would choose very carefully what tones I would choose because I knew that when I would play a note I would become that note.

Lorin Hollander

I carefully number the bricks of my heart for a later reconstruction.

Jeff Silva

Interviewer: "I've got lots of questions to ask you." Yogi Berra: "If you ask me anything I don't know, I'm not going to answer."

The American artist Chester Harding, painting Daniel Boone's portrait, asked the old frontiersman, then in his eighties, if he had ever been lost. Boone replied, "No, I can't say I was ever lost, but I was bewildered once for three days."

A little girl after hearing Beethoven's Ninth Symphony for the first time, asked, "What do we do now?"

If we live, we live; if we die, we die; if we suffer, we suffer; if we are terrified, we are terrified. There is no problem about it.

Alan Watts

A man's legs must be long enough to reach the ground.

Abraham Lincoln

How can a woman be expected to be happy with a man who insists on treating her as if she were a perfectly normal human being.

Oscar Wilde

Says yes when nobody asked.

Lao Proverb

Nothing is more conducive to peace of mind than not having any opinion at all.

G.C. Lichtenberg

The man who is unable to people his solitude is also unable to be alone in a busy crowd.

Charles Baudelaire

Because of you, I again seek out the signs that precipitate desires: shooting stars, falling objects.

Pablo Neruda

You see, when weaving a blanket, an Indian woman leaves a flaw in the weaving of that blanket to let the soul out.

Martha Graham

I'm going to make you think about me every minute of the day. I put a picture of you behind the door and I stuck two pins in your eyes. Now you're going to think about me for the rest of your life because the pins have fallen out of the picture.

Gabriel Maria Marquez

We all want to be famous people, and the moment we want to *be* something we are no longer free.

Krishnamurti

There's no present. There's only the immediate future and the recent past.

George Carlin

True singing, Rilke says, does not involve the attempt to accomplish something, to become a better person, to achieve salvation, or to publish a book. "Real singing is a different movement of air. Air moving around nothing."

One day, someone showed me a glass of water that was half full. And he said, "Is it half full or half empty?" So I drank the water. No more problem.

Alexander Jodorowsky

A prince had once told the Princess the moon was a white pearl caught in a fishnet of stars, or that it was a slice of melon eaten away by the souls of the dead. "Make up your mind!" she told him, "I happen to know it is a cabbage."

Anonymous

Not activity. Not reasoning. Not calculating. Not busy behavior of any kind. Not reading. Not talking. Not making an effort. Not thinking. Simply bearing in mind what it is one needs to know.

G. Spencer Brown

When we dream that we dream, we are beginning to wake up.

Novalis

"How do you teach, 'is the world round or flat?'" The teacher looked for some hint of the desired answer. Finding none, he finally said: "I can teach it either way."

Newspaper

What is here is elsewhere: what is not here is nowhere.

Vishvassara Tantra

I am for the art of things lost.

Claes Oldenburg

People who have their feet planted firmly on the ground often have difficulty getting their pants off.

Anonymous

When the Nandi men are away on a foray, nobody at home may pronounce the names of the absent warriors; they must be referred to as birds.

Sir James Frazer

Love, she said, should be said more slowly, and ran from the house. Words could not catch her as such. Honesty is so slow, that is the trouble.

Author Unknown

Those great Italian primitives exported by American collectors after the war were covered by atrocious 'modern' paintings which the collector would then order his restorer in New York to scrape off, revealing the masterpiece beneath (thus evading customs at both the Italian and American ends). One such collector, after some delay, sent his restorer a worried telegram: HOW ARE YOU GETTING ON? The reply came back, HAVE REMOVED FUTURISTIC DAUB, SCRAPED OFF FAKE DUCCIO, AM DOWN TO PORTRAIT OF MUSSOLINI, WHERE DO I STOP?

Hugh Vickers and Caroline McCullough

There are no stupid questions, only stupid answers.

Anonymous

Why do we treasure so highly our moment of being that flutters away like leaves of the laurel, darker than all surrounding green? Not because happiness is true, that unearned profit of certain loss.

Rainer Maria Rilke

Don't just do something, Buddha said, stand there!

Daniel Berrigan

What can be said, lacks reality. Only what fails to make its way into words exists and counts.

E.M. Cioran

At each mile, each year, old men with closed faces point out the road to children with gestures of reinforced concrete.

Jacques Prevert

They will say you are on the wrong road, if it is your own.

Antonio Porchia

The capacity to blunder slightly is the real marvel of DNA. Without this special attribute, we would still be anaerobic bacteria and there would be no music.

Lewis Thomas

Now my own suspicion is that the universe is not only queerer than we suppose, but queerer than we can suppose.

J.B.S. Haldane

People who look through keyholes are apt to get the idea that most things are keyhole shaped.

Anonymous

I'm afraid that if you look at a thing long enough, it loses all of its meaning.

Andy Warhol

A man is privileged when his passion obliges him to betray his convictions to please the woman he loves.

René Magritte

On the contrary, I am bored, but it's my duty to be attentive.

Frank O'Hara

Yet Auric himself once told me that in scoring *Blood of A Poet* he produced what is commonly known as love music for love scenes, game music for game scenes, funeral music for funeral scenes. Cocteau had the bright idea of replacing the love music with the funeral, game music with love, funeral with game. And it worked—like prosciutto and melon.

Ned Rorem

I have a simple philosophy: Fill what's empty. Empty what's full. Scratch where it itches.

Alice Roosevelt Longworth

Anything which is really new to us is by that fact automatically traditional.

T.S. Eliot

The love we give away is the only love we keep.

Elbert Hubbard

Animals studied by Americans rush about frantically, with an incredible display of hustle and pep, and at last achieve the desired result by chance. Animals observed by Germans sit still and think, and at last evolve the solution out of their inner consciousness.

Bertrand Russell

Those who gave away their wings are sad not to see them fly.

Antonio Porchia

It was so cold I almost got married.

Shelley Winters

Policeman Gilhaney was on his bicycle forty-eight percent of the time. Therefore, as you can plainly see, atoms of the bicycle slowly migrated into Gilhaney and atoms of Gilhaney slowly migrated into the bicycle. It was an explanation of why Irish policemen, like bicycles, could be leaned up against a wall, and why bicycles were often found in kitchens where there had been a mysterious disappearance of pie.

Author Unknown

It goes without saying that as soon as one cherishes the thought of winning the contest or displaying one's skill in technique, swordsmanship is doomed.

Takano Shigeyoshi

Dr. Miller says we are pessimistic because life seems like a very bad, very screwed-up film. If you ask "What the hell is wrong with the projector?" and go up to the control room, you find it's empty. You *are* the projectionist, and you should have been up there all the time.

Colin Wilson

A beautiful woman who is pleasing to men is good only for frightening fish when she falls into the water.

Zen Proverb

Johnson and Boswell were together at a concert in which some violin virtuoso had just sweated through a very difficult piece. Boswell said, "That piece must have been very difficult." Johnson answered, "Difficult? I wish it had been impossible!"

Raymond Smullyan

Cloquet hated reality but realized it was
still the only place to get a good steak.

Woody Allen

What I am is so real it dies on my lips.

Author Unknown

Invent a past for the present.

Daniel Stern

Solitaire, precisely ... I'm a realist.

Jean Renoir

Realism is a bad word. In a sense
everything is realistic. I see no line between
the imaginary and the real.

Federico Fellini

A little boy came home and told his
mother he had gotten first prize in an
examination. The question had been, "How
many legs has a horse?" He had answered
"Three." When his mother asked how he had
gotten the first prize, he replied that all the
other children had said "Two."

Long only for what you have.

Andre Gide

Who then tells a finer tale than any of us.
Silence does.

Isak Dinesen

It is interesting to speculate how different the world must have looked before Thomas Gray coined the word 'picturesque' in 1740 or before Whewell coined 'scientist' in the 19th century, or before Shakespeare coined the words 'assassination', 'disgraceful', or 'lonely'.

How old would you be if you didn't know how old you was?

Satchell Paige

Working with Hitchcock early in her career, actress Ingrid Bergman was uncomfortable about the way he had asked her to play a certain scene. "I don't think I can do that naturally" she told him and went on to explain her difficulties and suggest possible alternatives. Hitchcock listened solemnly, nodding from time to time: Miss Bergman felt she had made her case. "All right," he finally said, "if you can't do it naturally, then *fake* it."

Clifton Fadiman

Robert Graves once said that the supreme gift bestowed on the poet by the Muse was that of poetic humour, and that in its final draft, a poem would become so perfectly ambivalent as to make him wonder whether the insertion of a simple "not" wouldn't perhaps improve it.

The Sunday Times

Man is air in the air and in order to become a point in the air he has to fall.

Antonio Porchia

The puzzle of the numerous minutely different crowds of atoms with competing claims to be one table.

Peter Geach

Life is too important a thing ever to talk seriously about it.

Oscar Wilde

Truth only reveals itself when one gives up all preconceived ideas.

Shoseki

I have learned that only two things are necessary to keep one's wife happy. First, let her think she's having her own way. And second, let her have it.

Lyndon Baines Johnson

If you won't leave me alone, I'll find someone who will.

Author Unknown

"Where you headed from here?" "I don't know." "Can't get lost then." (conversation in Nameless, Tennessee)

William Least Heat Moon

What we owe to the silence makes our ripening exact.

Rainer Maria Rilke

Two monks were arguing about the temple flag. One said the flag moved, the other said the wind moved. Master Eno overheard them and said, "It is neither the wind nor the flag, but your mind that moves."

There is only the boat floating in nothing,
in the dark, without directions, without size,
you cannot feel it, you cannot smell it. You
cannot taste it. Then it has gone. Then
nothing has gone. The voice must have
come. Because it has gone.

W.S. Merwin

One is not likely to doubt that two plus two
equals four until one begins to think about
clouds in the sky, which merge and separate
as the wind propels them. Do two ideas plus
two ideas always make four ideas?

Author Unknown

And once when saying his prayers, which
he (Sidney Smith) always did out loud, he
was overheard to say: "Now, Lord, I'll tell
you an anecdote."

Patrick Mahoney

Spooks can't stand endurance.

Richard Kehl

Perhaps everything terrible is in its
deepest being something helpless that wants
help from us.

Rainer Maria Rilke

The art of living is the art of knowing how to believe lies.

Cesare Pavese

When smashing monuments, save the pedestals -- they always come in handy.

Stanislaw J. Lec

After watching many planes fly over her home, a child was boarding a plane for the first time. Turning to her mother, she whispered, "When do we get smaller?"

Author Unknown

The terror is, all promises are kept. Even happiness.

Author Unknown

The day I was imprisoned I had a small pencil which I used up within a week. If you ask the pencil it will say – "My whole lifetime." If you ask me, I'll say, "So what? Only a week."

Author Unknown

And yet his grief is a great guide through
this world. Even, perhaps, the surest of
guides. As long as guides are needed.

W. S. Merwin

In orbiting the sun, the earth departs from
a straight line by only one-ninth of an inch
every eighteen miles—a very straight line in
human terms. If the orbit changed by one
tenth of an inch every eighteen miles, our
orbit would be vastly larger and we would all
freeze to death. One-eighth of an inch? We
would all be incinerated.

Science Digest

Andres Segovia once said his interest in
the guitar began when he was eight years
old. "One day a man walked by me in the
street playing a guitar. He put my fingers on
the strings and I played, not as if I were
learning but as if I were remembering."

If I could learn the word for yes it could
teach me questions.

W. S. Merwin

I do not pin the least butterfly of life on importance.

André Breton

But he wanted you to be proud of him, so he invented the telephone before he called.

Peter Klappert

If you haven't any lines in this scene with Kite, you must find reasons for saying nothing.

William Gaskill with stage instructions.

To live for memory, forgetting almost all.

Jorge Luis Borges

Cuskoy, a town in eastern Turkey, is called the "bird village" with good reason. Its inhabitants have perfected a language system of chirps, tweets, and twitters almost indistinguishable from authentic bird sounds. The people of Cuskoy developed this unique system because of a ravine and a river which bisect their village and an almost daily fog that prevents the use of hand signals.

Charles Berlitz

If I were about to start to build a platform, I think I'd start with ash.

Cynthia MacDonald

If the butterflies in your stomach die, send yellow death announcements.

Yoko Ono

It is a tremendous act of violence to begin anything. I am not able to begin. I simply skip what should be the beginning.

Rainer Maria Rilke

It requires a very unusual mind to undertake the analysis of the obvious.

Alfred North Whitehead

And see, no longer blinded by our eyes.

Rupert Brooke

David Niven's first wife died when she was killed by falling down some cellar steps whilst playing "Sardines" at a Hollywood dinner party and has attributed to her the most politely touching last words ever uttered, "They'll never ask us again."

Life must be understood backwards. But it must be lived forward.

Soren Kierkegaard

When I was younger I could remember anything, whether it had happened or not.

Mark Twain

One of the definitions of sanity is the ability to tell real from unreal. Soon we'll need a new definition.

Alvin Toffler

I never met anyone so absent-minded as Professor Sylvester, the great mathematician. One afternoon, just as I was going for a walk, he handed me an ink-bottle, begging me to drop it in the letter-box, as he was anxious to have an immediate answer.

Henrietta Corkran

"Things have to be in sequence," I say. "A has to go before B." "Yes, but there's something that goes before A!"

Shana Alexander

Art to me was a state: it didn't need to be an accomplishment.

Margaret Anderson

In some basic way, I have always really felt, in my more rational and intelligent moments, that there is something tremendously creative about truancy.

Jonathan Miller

There's an excellent profile in *Interview* in which Jeanne Moreau says: "I shall die very young." "How young?" they ask her.
"I don't know, maybe seventy, maybe eighty, maybe ninety. But I shall be very young."

by way of Diana Vreeland

We have to sleep with open eyes, we must dream with our hands.

Octavio Paz

And you are left, to no one belonging wholly, not so dark as a silent house, nor quite so surely pledged unto eternity as that which grows and climbs the night.

Rainer Maria Rilke

There is another world, but it is in this one.

Paul Eluard

Steps being taken to keep fireflies from going out.

Newspaper Headline

Jung-kwang asks, "How much does this glass of water weigh?" Puzzled, I reply, "I don't know. Half a pound or so."
Jung-kwang slaps his hand on the table and laughs. "Are you still measuring?"

Author Unknown

She is such a good friend that she would throw all her acquaintances into the water for the pleasure of fishing them out.

Talleyrand

You cannot compare this present experience with a past experience. You can only compare it with a memory of the past, which is a part of the present experience.

Alan Watts

The French painter Rousseau was once asked why he put a naked woman on a red sofa in the middle of his jungle pictures. He answered, "I needed a bit of red there."

Reality is not always probable, or likely.

Jorge Luis Borges

Anything capable of being believed is an image of truth.

William Blake

Albert Speer survived in prison partly by persisting in a series of elaborate games, creations that he describes as "the organization of emptiness." He converted his walks around the prison yard into a walk around the world, studying guidebooks and charting on a map his progress across Afghanistan, up the coast of China. One day, while promenading with Hess, Speer startled his companion by suddenly announcing that they were only an hour from the Bering Strait.

On one day in the week, if possible,
neither read nor write poetry.

Chinese rule of health

The Duke of Cambridge protested that he
wasn't against change. He favored it, he
said, when there was no alternative.

How could I be anything but a dissenter?
Who wants the opinion of a group?

Saul Bellow

Meeting a friend in a corridor, Wittgenstein
said: "Tell me, why do people always say it
was *natural* for men to assume that the sun
went round the earth rather than that the
earth was rotating?" His friend said, "Well,
obviously, because it just *looks* as if the sun
is going round the earth." To which the
philosopher replied, "Well, what would it
have looked like if it had looked as if the
earth was rotating?"

Never speak more clearly than you think.

Jeremy Bernstein

That theory is worthless. It isn't even wrong!

Wolfgang Pauli

The notes I handle no better than many pianists. But the pauses between the notes-- ah, that is where the art resides.

Artur Schnabel

Tell me how your hands fall and I will tell you what you will wave to next.

W.S. Merwin

The only trouble with the future is it gets here so much faster than it used to.

Author Unknown

Max Ernst used to describe how, as a child, he would watch his father painting in the back garden. One day Ernst Senior was stymied by a tree that he could not paint satisfactorily, so, to the outrage of his son the budding surrealist, he fetched an axe and chopped it down, editing it from both life and art.

Robert Hughes

My whole work from a career point of view has been to try to abandon what I knew how to do.

Milton Glaser

He who goes up step by step always finds himself level with a step.

Antonio Porchia

All great work is preparing yourself for the accident to happen.

Sidney Lumet

Be careful where you aim. You might get there.

Chet Atkins

Consider 3,844. "For you it's just a three and an eight and a four," said William Klein to Smith, who considers Klein the world's greatest living mental calculator. "But I say, 'Hi, sixty-two squared.' "

I wish I could have known earlier that you have all the time you'll need right up to the day you die.

William Wiley

In fact, I've come to the conclusion that I never did know anything about it.

Thomas Edison, on electricity.

Schiller wrote best when smelling rotting apples, Zola was stimulated by the ambience of artificial light, even at midday; the naturalist, Comte de Buffon, felt inspired only when dressed as if for a social event; Ben Johnson responded to the influences of tea, the purring of a cat, and the odor of orange peel; and Andre Gretry composed with his feet in ice water. Einstein and Freud both worked particularly well during bouts of abdominal discomfort (though neither deliberately induced such distress as an aid to creativity).

No one can make you feel inferior without your consent.

Eleanor Roosevelt

I am so wise I had my mouth sewn shut.

John Berryman

Two parallel lines meet somewhere in infinity...and they believe it ... .

G. C. Lichtenberg

I remembered a story of how Bach was approached by a young admirer one day and asked, "But Papa Bach, how do you manage to think of all these new tunes?" "My dear fellow," Bach is said to have answered, according to my version, "I have no need to think of them. I have the greatest difficulty not to step on them when I get out of bed in the morning and start moving around my room."

Laurens Van der Post

Everything is a little bit of darkness, even the light.

Antonio Porchia

As for myself, ever since I was born I have struggled with my puzzling conviction that everything is simultaneous.

John Berger

The famous French soldier Marshall Lyautey asked his gardener to plant a row of trees of a certain rare variety in his garden the next morning. The gardener said he would be glad to do so, but he cautioned the Marshall that trees of this size take a century to grow to full size. "In that case," replied Lyautey, "plant them this afternoon."

Douglas Hofstader

Like a harp burning on an island nobody knows about.

James Tate

I shall be a dawn made of all the air I ever breathed.

Saint Geraud

During his years of poverty Balzac lived in an unheated and almost unfurnished garret. On one of the bare walls the writer inscribed the words: "rosewood paneling with commode;" on another: "Gobelin tapestry with Venetian mirror;" and in the place of honor over the empty fireplace: "Picture by Raphael."

E. Fuller

The artist Leon Kroll was having trouble with a seascape. "My boy," said Winslow Homer, "if you want to make a great sea, use only two waves."

The today that never comes on time.

Octavio Paz

A teacher asks the boy what two plus two equals. "Four," the child responds. "Very good, Robert." "Very good!" the child says indignantly. "Very good! It's perfect."

Newspaper

I remember a medicine man in Africa who said to me almost with tears in his eyes: "We have no dreams anymore since the British are in the country." When I asked him why, he answered: "The District Commissioner knows everything."

Carl Jung

Don' t think, but look.

Ludwig Wittgenstein

Our alphabet's first sound is but the lengthening of a sigh.

Joseph Brodsky

It's illegal in Salem, Virginia to leave the house without knowing where you intend to go.

Newspaper

Some years ago a young scholar who greatly admired A. E. Houseman's work wrote to the poet and asked him how he managed always to select the right word. Houseman replied that he didn't bother trying to get the right word, he simply bothered about getting rid of the wrong one.

Do fireflies burn you if they fly into you?

Vladimir Nabokov

Yes, I will go. I would rather grieve over your absence than over you.

Antonio Porchia

The game of golf would lose a great deal if croquet mallets and billiard cues were allowed on the putting green.

Ernest Hemingway

During a visit to Venice, Duchamp sat on the Piazza San Marco, smoking a cigar, while Teeny (his wife) went upstairs to a museum. Every once in a while, she would lean out of the window and describe what she was seeing.

told by Merce Cunningham

One morning after the war had just ended I visited Alberto Giacometti in his hotel room. He was to return to Paris the next day. I asked him: "Have you shipped your sculptures yet?" He replied: "No, I'm taking them with me." He pulled six matchboxes from his pockets. In them was the work of those years.

Albert Skira

Eschew the monumental. Shun the epic. All the guys who can paint great big pictures can paint great small ones.

Ernest Hemingway

She is hard to tempt as everything seems to please her equally.

Anne Raymo

For some people, style is a very complicated way of saying very simple things: for others, it is a very simple way of saying very complicated things.

Jean Cocteau

What if your knees bent the other way, what would a chair look like?

Anonymous

Perfection is laziness.

John Cage

Once when I was in Elaine de Kooning's studio, at a time when the metal sculptor Herbert Ferber occupied the studio immediately above, there came through the floor a most horrible crashing and banging. "What in the world is that?" I asked, and Elaine said, "Oh, that's Herbert thinking."

Donald Barthelme

Another way of approaching the thing is to consider it unnamed, unnameable.

Francis Ponge

We do survive every moment, after all, except the last one.

John Updike

Real generosity toward the future consists in giving all to what is present.

Marcel Camus

The three sisters were drawing all kinds of things beginning with the letter 'M': but could they draw *all* kinds? The Dormouse says they draw "mouse-traps, and the moon, and memory, and muchness – you know you say things are 'much of a muchness' – did you ever see such a thing as a drawing of a muchness?"

Lewis Carroll

By daily dying I have come to be.

Theodore Roethke

Neurophysiologists will not likely find what they are looking for outside their own consciousness, for that which they are looking for is that which is looking.

Keith Floyd

Mallarme thought it was the job of poetry, using words, to clean up our word-clogged reality by creating silences around things.

Man's maturity: to have regained the seriousness that he had as a child at play.

Friedrich Nietzsche

What's beautiful in science is that same thing that's beautiful in Beethoven. There's a fog of events and suddenly you see a connection. It connects things that were always in you that were never put together before.

Victor Weisskopf

I love being a writer. What I can't stand is the paperwork.

Peter De Vries

Sometimes I've believed as many as six impossible things before breakfast.

Lewis Carroll

Oscar Wilde, on his deathbed, was drifting in and out of consciousness. Once when he opened his eyes he was heard to murmur, "This wallpaper is killing me; one of us has got to go."

The observer, when he seems to himself to be observing a stone, is really, if physics is to be believed, observing the effects of the stone upon himself.

Bertrand Russell

Now, what is it which makes a scene interesting? If you see a man coming through a doorway, it means nothing. If you see him coming through a window – that is at once interesting.

Billy Wilder

Living is entirely too time-consuming.

Irene Peter

It is a far, far better thing to have a firm anchor in nonsense than to put out on the troubled seas of thought.

John Kenneth Galbraith

_Further
Departures_

Alfred Tennyson became interested in Persian literature and began to study the language, intending to translate the poetry of Hafez. But his wife thought the characters of the Persian alphabet were "peculiar" and harmful to his eyes. When she discovered also that Persian was written from right to left, she became convinced that his eyesight would suffer irreparable damage. So she hid all his Persian textbooks and persuaded him to take up badminton instead.

William Shawcross

An artist never really finishes his work; he merely abandons it.

Paul Valery

Anything simple always interests me.

David Hockney

When I am working on a problem, I never think about beauty. I think only how to solve the problem. But when I have finished, if the solution is not beautiful, I know it is wrong.

Buckminster Fuller

Have the courage to live. Anyone can die.

Robert Cody

I asked Ring Lardner the other day how he writes his short stories, and he said he wrote a few widely separated words or phrases on a piece of paper and then went back and filled in the spaces.

Harold Ross

In the course of my labors I suddenly stumble upon something unexpected. This unexpected element strikes me. I make a note of it. An accident is perhaps the only thing that really inspires us.

Igor Stravinsky

Speed kills colour...the gyroscope, when turning at full speed, shows up gray.

Paul Morand

"Is there any point to which you would wish to draw my attention?"
"To the curious incident of the dog in the nighttime."
"The dog did nothing in the nighttime."
"That was the curious incident," remarked Sherlock Holmes.

Arthur Conan Doyle

Man sees and moves in what he sees, but he sees only what he dreams.

Paul Valery

Without naiveté, there is no beauty.

Denis Diderot

The greatest explorer on this earth never takes voyages as long as those of the man who descends to the depth of his heart.

Julien Green

My propositions are elucidatory in this way: he who understands them finally recognizes them as senseless...whereof one cannot speak thereof one must be silent.

Ludwig Wittgenstein